Design: Jill Coote
Recipe Photography: Peter Barry
Jacket and Illustration Artwork: Jane Winton,
courtesy of Bernard Thornton Artists, London
Editors: Jillian Stewart, Kate Cranshaw and Laura Potts

CLB 3512
Published by Grange Books,
an imprint of Grange Books PLC,
The Grange, Grange Yard, London.
© 1994 CLB Publishing,
Godalming, Surrey, England.
All rights reserved.
Printed and bound in Singapore
Published 1994
ISBN 1-85627-409-8

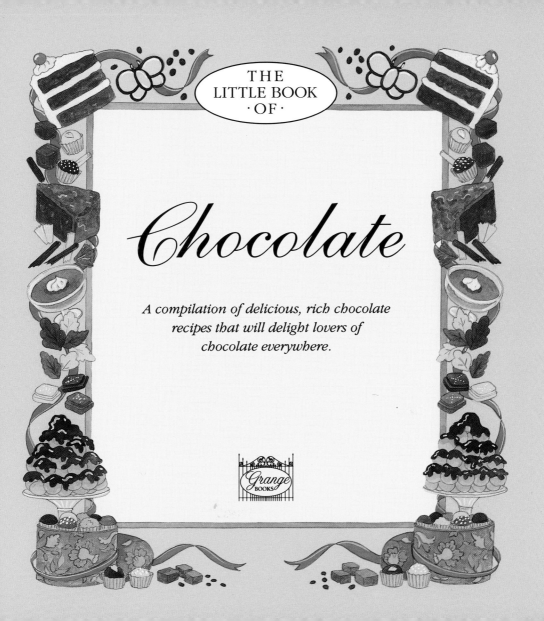

THE LITTLE BOOK ·OF·

Chocolate

*A compilation of delicious, rich chocolate
recipes that will delight lovers of
chocolate everywhere.*

Grange BOOKS

Introduction

*T*hough it has become common to hear people refusing to eat chocolate because they are fearful for their figure or because they believe that it contains too much sugar or caffeine, it is unusual to hear anyone refuse because they find the taste or the texture unpalatable. Certainly if someone expressed an actual dislike of chocolate, they would probably be regarded as something of an oddity. After all, what sort of person does *not* like chocolate? Whatever it is that makes them so addictive, the products of the humble cocoa bean have made an important mark on modern eating habits.

The cocoa bean made its first appearance in Europe in the sixteenth century, when Spanish explorers returned from the New World with the beans, and tales of how they were dried, ground and then mixed with water and spices by the native peoples to make a rich drink. Though early explorers spurned the drink, finding it too bitter, those who followed in their footsteps some sixty or seventy years later drank it with enthusiasm, and by the end of the sixteenth century the first processing plants were established in Spain. The new drink, which in its European form omitted all the additions found in the original version save sugar and vanilla, quickly grew in popularity.

For two centuries, chocolate was sold almost exclusively as a drink and contemporary recipe books feature very few recipes for confections made from the cocoa bean. This dearth of recipes had its root in the fact that chocolate paste did not combine well with sugar. A major breakthrough came with a development in the manufacturing process, known as the Dutch process. Developed as a way of making chocolate drinks lighter and less oily, the process used a press to remove the excess fat from the paste. As had been desired, the press created a substance – cocoa powder – which was finer in texture and less fatty when mixed with water or milk. It also produced cocoa butter. This could be combined with the untreated chocolate paste, or chocolate liquor, making it easier to combine with sugar and other ingredients.

There are several types of chocolate on the market which roughly speaking can be divided up into five categories, unsweetened or baking chocolate, bittersweet or semi-sweet chocolate, sweet chocolate and milk chocolate, white chocolate (which contains quantities of cocoa butter but no cocoa solids) and finally couverture, which is used for dripping or coating. The different varieties of chocolate are made by combining the chocolate liquor with different percentages of cocoa butter and adding sugar and flavourings.

The recipes collected in this book include some all-time favourites, among them Chocolate Brownies, Chocolate Ice Cream, Chocolate Fudge and Chocolate Profiteroles. Each utterly delicious recipe is accompanied by clear, step-by-step instructions, explaining some of the techniques used when cooking with chocolate and giving useful tips on how to get the very best results. A delight for anyone with a sweet tooth, this book is a must for any dedicated chocolate lover.

Vienna Cake

SERVES 8-10

A versatile cake which can be adapted to suit any occasion.

PREPARATION: 20 mins
COOKING: 1½ hrs

225g/8oz butter or margarine
225g/8oz Barbados sugar
3 eggs, separated
3 tbsps milk
90g/3oz cocoa powder
225g/8oz plain flour
175g/6oz plain chocolate

---

1. Place the butter and sugar in a mixing bowl and cream together until light and fluffy.

2. Add the egg yolks and beat well. Mix in the milk.

3. Combine the cocoa powder with the flour and fold into the creamed mixture, which will be very stiff at this point.

4. Beat the egg whites until they are stiff and fold gently into the mixture.

5. Spoon into a lined 18cm/7-inch cake tin and bake in an oven preheated to 150°C/300°F/Gas Mark 2 for 1½ hours, until a skewer inserted into the centre comes out clean.

6. Turn out onto a wire rack to cool.

7. When the cake is completely cold, melt the chocolate in a bowl over a pan of simmering water.

8. Cover the cake with the melted chocolate, smoothing it over with a knife dipped in boiling water.

9. Leave to harden before storing in an airtight tin.

Chocolate Ice Cream

SERVES 4

A smooth chocolate ice cream made from a rich egg custard sauce.

PREPARATION: 30 mins, plus freezing

6 egg yolks
120g/4oz sugar
520ml/18 fl oz milk
30g/4 tbsps cocoa powder

1. Whisk the egg yolks and sugar together until pale and thick.

2. Bring the milk to the boil in a large saucepan.

3. Whisk in the egg mixture, reduce the heat and whisk continuously until the mixture thickens.

4. Once the sauce is thick, remove from the heat and stir in the cocoa powder.

5. Pour the mixture into the bowl of an ice cream maker and set in motion.*

6. Once the ice cream has crystallized it can be spooned into a container and kept in the freezer until needed.

*If an ice cream maker is not available, pour the mixture into a shallow tray and place in the freezer until mushy. Remove from the freezer and beat the mixture. Refreeze, beat thoroughly, pour into a covered container and freeze until firm.

Chocolate Apple Cake

MAKES 1× 18CM/8-INCH CAKE

This cake is nicer if kept in an airtight tin for a day before serving.

PREPARATION: 25 mins
COOKING: 1¼ hrs

150g/5oz butter, softened or soft margarine
120g/4oz light muscavado sugar
1 large egg, beaten
175g/6oz fine wholemeal flour
90g/3oz cocoa powder
1½ tsps baking powder
1 tbsp Amontillado sherry
400g/14oz Bramley cooking apples, peeled and
　　sliced

Topping
120g/4oz chocolate chips
Knob of butter
A little water

1. Cream the butter and sugar together until fluffy.

2. Add half of the beaten egg and continue creaming.

3. Fold in the rest of the egg together with the sieved flour, cocoa and baking powder and sherry.

4. Place half of the mixture into a round 18cm/8-inch cake tin and cover with the sliced apples.

5. Add the other half of the mixture and smooth the top.

6. Bake in an oven preheated to 160°C/325°F/Gas Mark 3, for 1¼ hours or until firm to the touch.

7. Melt the chocolate chips with the butter and water and drizzle over the top of the cake.

Crêpes au Chocolat et Framboises

SERVES 6

Crêpes Suzette may be more famous, but these, filled with chocolate and raspberry, are incredibly delicious.

PREPARATION: 30 mins
COOKING: 30 mins

Crêpe Batter
420ml/¾ pint milk and water mixed
4 eggs
Pinch salt
225g/8oz plain flour, sifted
1 tbsp sugar
60g/2oz melted butter or oil

Filling
225g/8oz plain chocolate, grated
120g/4oz seedless raspberry jam
Whipped cream and chopped, roasted
   hazelnuts

1. Put all the ingredients for the crêpes into a food processor or blender and process for about 1 minute, pushing down the sides occasionally. Process a few seconds more to blend thoroughly.

2. Leave, covered, in a cool place for 30 minutes to 1 hour. The consistency of the batter should be that of thin cream. Add more milk if necessary.

3. Brush a crêpe pan or small frying pan lightly with oil and place over high heat. When a slight haze forms, pour a large spoonful of the batter into the pan and swirl the pan to cover the base.

4. Pour out any excess into a separate bowl. Cook on one side until just beginning to brown around the edges.

5. Turn over and cook on the other side until lightly speckled with brown. Slide each crêpe onto a plate and repeat using the remaining batter.

6. Reheat the pan occasionally in between cooking each crêpe. The amount of batter should make 12 crêpes.

7. As the crêpes are cooked, sprinkle them evenly with grated chocolate and divide the raspberry jam among all the crêpes. Roll them up so that the jam shows at the ends, or fold into triangles.

8. Reheat in an oven preheated to 180°C/350°F/Gas Mark 4, for about 10 minutes before serving. Top with whipped cream and a sprinkling of roasted hazelnuts.

Jamaican Mousse Cake

SERVES 6-8

This delectable chocolate mousse cake is sure to tempt even the most strong willed of dieters, so be warned!

PREPARATION: 25 mins, plus chilling

175g/6oz plain chocolate
3 tbsps dark rum
280ml/½ pint double cream
15g/½oz soft brown sugar
1 tbsp hot strong black coffee
2 large bananas, peeled and mashed until smooth
3 eggs, separated
Chocolate curls, to decorate

1. Put the chocolate into a bowl and melt it over a pan of hot water.

2. Stir the rum and half of the cream into the chocolate and beat thoroughly until smooth.

3. Dissolve the sugar in the coffee. Put the mashed bananas into a large bowl and beat in the coffee and sugar mixture.

4. Add the egg yolks to the banana mixture and beat well. Continue beating and add all the chocolate mixture.

5. Whisk the egg whites until they form stiff peaks.

Step 6
Quickly, but carefully fold the egg whites into the chocolate mixture with a metal spoon.

6. Quickly, but carefully, fold the whisked egg whites into the chocolate and banana mixture.

7. Spoon the mixture into a lightly greased and base-lined springform cake tin. Chill for at least 2 hours, or until completely set and firm.

8. Carefully loosen the sides of the mousse cake with a warmed round bladed knife and unmould the sides of the tin.

9. Carefully slide the mousse off the base of the tin onto a serving plate.

10. Whip the remaining cream until it is thick and pipe a decorative border on the mousse cake.

11. Sprinkle over the chocolate curls and chill well before serving.

Chocolate Charlotte

SERVES 4

Impress the chocolate-lovers in your life with this rich confection.

PREPARATION: 30 mins, plus chilling

175g/6oz plain chocolate
120ml/4 fl oz double cream
3 tbsps sugar
45g/1½oz butter
4 eggs, separated
16 sponge fingers
2 tbsps rum
60ml/4 tbsps water

1. Combine the chocolate, cream, sugar and butter in a bowl. Place the bowl over a pan of hot water to melt the ingredients.

Step 2 Add the egg yolks one at a time, beating after each addition.

Step 3 Fold the stiffly-beaten egg whites into the chocolate mixture.

2. Once melted, remove from the heat and beat together well, adding the egg yolks one at a time and beating after each addition to incorporate thoroughly.

3. Beat the egg whites until very stiff, then fold carefully into the chocolate mixture.

4. Cut each sponge finger in half crosswise. Mix together the rum and water. Dip each biscuit half quickly into the mixture.

5. Use the dipped biscuits to line four individual charlotte molds. Pour one quarter of the chocolate mixture into the centre of each lined mold. Chill for about 6 hours in the refrigerator, or until set.

Devil's Food Cake

MAKES 1 CAKE
Serve this with whipped cream to be truly devilish.

PREPARATION: 45 mins
COOKING: 40 mins

120g/4oz plain chocolate
225ml/8 fl oz milk
120g/4oz sugar
120g/4oz butter
3 eggs, separated
½ tsp vanilla essence
225g/8oz plain flour
2 tsps baking powder

Frosting
120g/4oz icing sugar
45g/1½oz cocoa powder
60g/2oz butter
45ml/3 tbsps water
75g/2½ caster sugar

---

1. Put the chocolate, half the milk and the sugar in a bowl over a pan of hot water and cook, stirring, until the chocolate has melted.

2. Beat the butter until soft, then beat in the egg yolks one at a time. Add the vanilla essence to the remaining milk, and sift the flour and baking powder together.

3. Gradually add the flour and milk mixtures alternately to the butter mixture, beating well after each addition to obtain a smooth mixture. Stir in the chocolate mixture.

4. Whisk the egg whites until stiff, then fold them gently into the cake mixture. Pour this into a greased deep 20cm/8-inch cake tin.

5. Bake for about 35 minutes, in an oven preheated to 180°C/350°F/Gas Mark 4, until a skewer inserted into the centre of the cake comes out clean. Turn out onto a rack to cool.

6. To make the frosting, sift the icing sugar and cocoa into a bowl. Put the butter, water and caster sugar into a saucepan and stir over a low heat until the sugar dissolves.

7. Bring to the boil then immediately pour into the centre of the dry ingredients. Beat with a wooden spoon until smooth.

8. Stir the icing occasionally until thick enough to leave a trail. Spread all over the cake and decorate by roughing-up with the tip of a table knife.

Mousse au Chocolat Basque

SERVES 6

This mousse is a dark chocolate mixture which sets to a rich cream in the refrigerator.

PREPARATION: 20 mins
COOKING: 10 mins

175g/6oz plain chocolate
75ml/2½ fl oz water
15g/½oz butter
2 tbsps rum
3 eggs, separated

1. Chop the chocolate into small pieces and combine with the water in a bowl over a pan of

Step 1 Melt the chopped chocolate with the water over a gentle heat.

Step 3 Fold lightly whipped egg whites into the chocolate mixture.

hot water. Cook over a very gentle heat so that the chocolate and water form a thick cream.

2. Remove from the heat, allow to cool slightly and then beat in the butter. Add the rum and beat in the egg yolks one at a time.

3. Whisk the egg whites until stiff but not dry and fold thoroughly into the chocolate mixture.

4. Pour into small pots or ramekins and chill overnight. Finish with whipped cream and chocolate curls to serve, if wished.

Chocolate Profiteroles

MAKES 18

These make the perfect dessert for a dinner party.

PREPARATION: 30 mins
COOKING: 30 mins

75g/2½oz strong plain flour
¼ tsp salt
60g/2oz butter, cut into small pieces
140ml/¼ pint cold water
2 eggs, well beaten
280ml/½ pint double cream, whipped
225g/8oz plain chocolate
3 tbsps cold water

---

1. Sift the flour and salt onto a piece of greaseproof paper. Put the butter and water in a saucepan over a medium heat. Bring to the boil.

2. Remove from the heat and immediately tip in all the flour. Beat vigorously with a wooden spoon until a smooth ball of paste forms and leaves the pan sides clean.

3. Gradually beat in the eggs until the mixture becomes less solid but resembles a stiff, glossy paste.

4. Grease 2 baking trays and pipe the mixture out into 18 small buns, using a piping bag fitted with a plain nozzle.

5. Bake in an oven preheated to 200°C/400°F/ Gas Mark 6, for 10 minutes and then raise the temperature to 220°C/425°F/Gas Mark 7 and cook for 15-20 minutes longer, or until light golden.

6. Remove from the oven and, with the handle of a teaspoon, pierce the side of each bun to allow the steam to escape. Return to the oven for 2 minutes, then cool on a wire rack.

7. Just before serving time, pipe the cream into the buns. Melt the chocolate and water in a bowl over hot water. Pour over the profiteroles and serve at once.

Sherry Cream Pie

MAKES 1 × 20cm/8-inch flan

This is a delicious and rich concoction which will be a favourite with everyone who tries it.

PREPARATION: 30 mins, plus chilling
COOKING: 35 mins

150g/5oz plain flour
60g/2oz caster sugar
90g/3oz butter, diced
1 egg yolk

Filling
225g/8oz plain chocolate, chopped or grated
3 tbsps medium sherry
1 tsp gelatine
4 eggs, separated

To Decorate
60g/2oz plain chocolate, melted
140ml/¼ pint double cream
1 tbsp sherry

1. Sieve the flour onto a work surface. Make a well in the centre and add the sugar, butter and egg yolk.

2. Mix these ingredients together with your fingertips, then gradually draw in the flour from the edge. If necessary add a little cold water.

3. Knead the dough until smooth, then wrap and chill for 30 minutes.

4. Lightly flour the work surface and roll out the dough; use to line a 20cm/8-inch loose-bottomed flan tin.

5. Prick the base of the flan with a fork. Line with greaseproof paper and baking beans.

6. Bake for 15 minutes in an oven preheated to 190°C/375°F/Gas Mark 5, then remove the paper and beans and bake for a further 15 minutes.

7. Remove the pastry case from the ring and leave to cool.

8. Put the chocolate, sherry and 2 tbsps cold water into a bowl over a pan of hot water. Sprinkle the gelatine over the top and stir gently over a low heat until it has dissolved.

9. Beat the egg yolks into the sauce, one at a time, and cool the mixture.

10. Whisk the egg whites until stiff but not dry and then fold it into the sauce. Pour the mixture into the flan case and chill until set.

11. To decorate, lightly whip the double cream. Divide the cream in half; stir the sherry into one half, and the melted chocolate into the other.

12. Fit two piping bags with star nozzles and fill each bag with a different cream. Decorate the top of the pie with alternate rosettes of the different creams.

Black Forest Gateau

SERVES 8-10

A classic favourite always bound to please.

PREPARATION: 35 mins
COOKING: 20-25 mins

6 eggs
225g/8oz caster sugar
1 tsp vanilla essence
120g/4oz plain chocolate, melted
120g/4oz flour, sieved

Syrup
60g/2oz sugar
75ml/5 tbsps water
2 tbsps kirsch

Filling
200g/7oz icing sugar
75g/2½oz unsalted butter
1 egg yolk
2 tbsps kirsch

Topping
275g/10oz drained, canned cherries
2 tbsps icing sugar
225ml/8 fl oz double cream, whipped
225g/8oz plain chocolate curls

1. Beat the eggs, sugar, and vanilla together for about 10 minutes until thick and fluffy. Alternately fold the melted chocolate and flour into the egg mixture, ending with some of the flour.

2. Pour the batter into 3 × 20cm/8-inch round cake tins that have been well-greased and floured. Bake in a preheated oven at 180°C/350°F/Gas Mark 4, for 10-15 minutes, or until a skewer inserted in centre comes out clean. Cool the cakes in the tins for 5 minutes; turn out onto racks to cool completely.

3. Mix together the sugar and water for the syrup and boil for 5 minutes. When cooled, stir in the kirsch. Prick the cake layers and pour the syrup over all three.

4. Beat together the sugar and butter for the filling until well-blended. Add the egg yolk and beat for 3-5 minutes or until light and fluffy, then fold in the kirsch.

5. To assemble the gateau spread one layer with the filling. Using 120g/4oz of the cherries, which have been patted dry, drop them evenly over the cream. Place the second layer on the cake. Repeat. Place the third layer on top.

6. Fold the icing sugar into the whipped cream and cover the sides and top of the cake. Decorate the top with the remaining cherries.

7. Press the chocolate curls onto the sides of the cake and sprinkle a few on top. Chill until serving time.

Chocolate Biscuit Cake

MAKES 16 squares
A very rich and delicious no-cook cake.

PREPARATION: 20-25 mins, plus chilling

225g/8oz rich tea biscuits
120g/4oz butter or margarine
1 tbsp brown sugar
3 tbsps cocoa powder
2 tbsps golden syrup
225g/8oz plain chocolate

1. Crush the biscuits into small pieces with a rolling pin and place in a mixing bowl.

2. Put the butter, sugar, cocoa powder and syrup into a pan and melt over a low heat, stirring all the time.

3. Add to the biscuit crumbs and mix together thoroughly.

4. Press the mixture into a 20cm/8-inch square container.

5. Break the chocolate into a heatproof bowl and place over a pan of simmering water until melted.

6. Cover the cake with the melted chocolate and mark it with the back of a fork.

7. Refrigerate until cold. Cut into squares and store in an airtight tin.

Chocolate Brownies

MAKES 16 squares

Rich, squidgy and delicious – a must for all chocoholics.

PREPARATION: 15 mins
COOKING: 35 mins

60g/2oz plain flour, sieved
Pinch salt
¼ tsp baking powder
120g/4oz plain chocolate
60g/2oz butter
2 eggs
225g/8oz sugar
90g/3oz walnuts, chopped

1. Sift the flour, salt and baking powder together in a bowl.

2. Melt the chocolate and butter in a bowl over a small saucepan of hot water.

3. Beat the eggs with the sugar for 2 minutes, until thick and pale.

4. Beat the melted chocolate into the egg mixture, then fold in the walnuts and flour.

5. Turn the mixture out into a greased and lined shallow 20cm/8-inch square tin and bake in an oven preheated to 160°C/325°F/Gas Mark 3 for 35 minutes.

6. Cut into squares while still warm and cool in the tin. Store in an airtight tin. Serve warm with cream or ice cream for a dessert.

Hazelnut Florentines

MAKES 24-30

Hazelnuts make a good alternative to almonds in these crisp, toffee-like biscuits.
They're a treat with coffee or ice cream.

PREPARATION: 45-50 mins
COOKING: 10 mins per batch

460g/1lb shelled and skinned hazelnuts
225g/8oz sugar
90ml/6 tbsps honey
90ml/6 tbsps double cream
225g/8oz butter
175g/6oz white chocolate, melted
175g/6oz plain chocolate, melted

---

1. Place the hazelnuts in a plastic bag and roughly crush them with a rolling pin.

2. Put the sugar, honey, cream and butter in a heavy-based saucepan and heat gently to dissolve the sugar. Bring to the boil and cook rapidly for about 1½ minutes. Remove from heat and stir in the nuts.

Step 4 Loosen partially-set Florentines with a palette knife.

Step 6 Use a skewer to make a decorative pattern in partially set chocolate.

3. Brush baking sheets well with oil and spoon out the mixture in even amounts. Make only about six Florentines at a time leaving plenty of space between each one.

4. Bake for about 10 minutes in a pre-heated 190°C/375°F/Gas Mark 5 oven. Allow to cool on the baking sheets and, when nearly set, loosen with a palette knife and transfer to a flat surface to cool completely.

5. When all the Florentines have been baked and cooled, melt both chocolates separately. Spread white chocolate on half of the Florentines and dark chocolate on the other half, or marble the two if preferred.

6. Place the biscuits chocolate side uppermost to cool slightly and then make a wavy pattern with a skewer, or swirl the chocolate with a knife until it sets in the desired pattern.

Chocolate Butter Sauce

MAKES 420ml/¾ pint
Delicious with ice-cream, fruit or pancakes.

PREPARATION: 5 mins
COOKING: 10 mins

225ml/8 fl oz water
225g/8oz plain chocolate, chopped
100g/3½oz butter, cut into small pieces
1 tbsp brandy

1. Put the water and the chocolate into a

Step 2 Drop the butter into the melted chocolate, piece by piece, stirring well until it has melted.

Step 3 Beat the brandy into the sauce, whisking until it is thick and glossy.

saucepan, and heat over a low heat, stirring until the chocolate has melted.

2. Remove from the heat and slowly stir in the butter, piece by piece, until the mixture becomes thick and glossy.

3. Whisk the brandy into the butter sauce and spoon into an attractive serving dish. This sauce can be served hot or cold.

Chocolate Truffles

MAKES about 30

These delicious truffles are ideal for serving after dinner or for giving as a special home-made present.

PREPARATION: 20 mins, plus chilling

175g/6oz (plain, milk or white) chocolate
15g/½oz butter or margarine
2 egg yolks
2 tsps brandy or black coffee
2 tsps single cream
3 tbsps each cocoa powder and ground
   almonds

---

1. Break the chocolate into pieces and melt in a bowl over a pan of simmering water. Stir in the butter or margarine.

2. Lightly beat the egg yolks and add to the

Step 4 Roll each piece of truffle mixture into a small ball.

Step 5 Gently roll the truffles in either the cocoa powder or the ground almonds.

chocolate, beating well until evenly incorporated.

3. Beat in the brandy or coffee and the cream and chill in the refrigerator for at least 1 hour or until firm.

4. Divide the mixture into about 30 even-sized pieces and roll these into small balls using your hands.

5. Put the cocoa powder and almonds onto separate plates and gently roll half the chocolates in each in one to coat.

6. Put the coated truffles into paper sweet cases and chill until required.

Chocolate Fudge

MAKES 680g/1½lbs

A quick and easy recipe which makes a lovely food present.

PREPARATION: 10 mins
COOKING: 8-10 mins

460g/1lb granulated sugar
90ml/6 tbsps milk
30g/1oz butter
175g/6oz plain chocolate, roughly chopped

---

1. Place the sugar and milk in a heavy-based saucepan and stir it forms until a paste.

2. Add the butter and chocolate and stir on a gentle heat until the chocolate has melted.

3. Slightly raise the heat and allow mixture to boil for 5 minutes.

4. Remove from the heat, beat well and pour into a well buttered 20cm/8-inch square tin.

5. Leave until cool and nearly set before cutting into squares. Store in an airtight container.

Collettes

MAKES 12

These attractive home-made sweets are ideal for serving at the end of a dinner party or formal meal.

PREPARATION: 40 mins, plus chilling

175g/6oz plain chocolate
60g/2oz white chocolate
2 tsps brandy or coffee essence
60ml/4 tbsps double cream
Chopped pistachio nuts, to decorate

---

1. Arrange 12 paper sweet cases on a tray or plate.

2. Break the plain chocolate into pieces and melt in a bowl over a pan of simmering water.

3. Using a small pastry or artists brush or a teaspoon, coat the inside of each paper case with an even layer of chocolate.

4. Thicken this layer gradually as the chocolate sets inside the case, by brushing extra thin layers over the top of the previous one.

Step 3 Using a small brush or teaspoon coat the insides of each paper case with an even layer of melted chocolate.

Step 9 Using a star nozzle, pipe swirls of the cream mixture into each chocolate shell.

5. Continue making the chocolate cases until all the melted chocolate has been used. Chill until the chocolate has set completely.

6. Melt the white chocolate in the same way as the plain chocolate. Stir in the brandy or coffee essence. Whip the cream until just holding its shape.

7. Carefully fold the cream into the chocolate mixture using a metal spoon. Mix well to blend evenly. Chill until just firm enough to pipe.

8. Carefully peel away the cases from the chocolate shells and put these into fresh paper cases to serve.

9. Place the cream mixture into a piping bag fitted with a 1cm/⅓-inch star nozzle. Pipe swirls of the mixture into the chocolate shells.

10. Sprinkle with chopped pistachio nuts and chill until required.

Index